With Stale Bread, You Make Bread Pudding!

With Stale Bread, You Make Bread Pudding!

My Childhood Among the People and Food of the Virginia Grill Restaurant

---

Stamatina P. Yocheved Samson, Ph.D.

Rich, Inspired, Fun, Leaves for Life.™

RIFLL PUBLISHING, INC.

Rifll Publishing, Inc.
P. O. Box 26, Trafalgar, IN 46181
editor@rifll.com
www.rifll.com

Samson, Stamatina P. Yocheved
   With stale bread, you make bread pudding! : My childhood among the
people and food of the Virginia Grill restaurant / Stamatina P. Yocheved
Samson

Summary: An immigrant-owned, working-man's, downtown middle-
America restaurant in the 1960s, is the real life stage for Dr. Samson's childhood recollections. Her father, Paul Vavul, immigrated from Greece to the
United States, settling in Indianapolis, Indiana. Functionally illiterate, he
created the Virginia Grill restaurant in 1939 with keen intelligence and street
savvy. In numerous display cases, patrons could view Mr. Vavul's collection
of guns—which he proclaimed the single largest in the Midwest, and centrally
featured on all promotional items. Dr. Samson tells us of being a child of
immigrants, and the range of characters she encountered at the restaurant,
both behind and in front of the counter—all from her unique, thoughtful, and
personable perspective. Her stories, along with her numerous black and white
photos, provide a fascinating window on civil rights era Indianapolis.

   ISBN: 978-1-935710-04-2

   1.Personal memoir—Biography & Autobiography 2.Midwest—United
States—History 3.Emigration & Immigration—Social Science 4.Business—
Biography & Autobiography   I.Title

CONTENTS

1. The Virginia Grill & the "Ethnic Rule" 1

2. A Child's Perspective 8

3. The Kitchen Crew 12

4. Lasting Impressions 17

Photos of gun collection 21

5. Honestly, Occasionally Something
   Funny Does Happen with Guns . 28

6. The Police and the Grill 30

7. About Paul 36

8. More About Paul 40

9. "Behind Every Great Man
   is a Great Woman" 43

10. May in Indianapolis 47

11. Marketing Marketing Marketing! 54

12. Days in the Life 60

13. Finding Solace in the Neighborhood 64

14. My First Uniform 66

15. What Happened to the Guns 69

16. The Tour 72

    About the Author 79

    Source of Gun Identifications 81

Chapter 1

The Virginia Grill and the "Ethnic Rule"

Everyone in his small Grecian village knew Paul Vavul was destined to be somewhere else in the world when, as a very young man, he melted his mother's precious sterling silver down for buck shot.

People often immigrate to another country in order to follow their dreams. Thus was the case with Paul. His parents were not terribly unhappy when at age fourteen, he sailed to the United States of America to join his brother, George.

The two brothers knocked around the United States for several years. They learned to speak the language and learned the business anywhere they worked. They were employed in odd jobs and in many, many restaurants. George settled in Chicago, Illinois while Paul settled in Indianapolis, Indiana.

The restaurant business had hooked Paul. He

was particularly fond of a place in Chicago called The Virginia Grill, and he always said he wanted to have his own place some day.

"Someday" came for Paul Vavul in 1939 when a new Virginia Grill opened on the busy East Washington Street, less than two miles from the very center of Indianapolis. Paul Vavul was the owner/founder of this new Virginia Grill.

Fifteen years later, in 1954, Paul married Mary Kargakos and she became a co-owner of the Grill. I came along the following year (1955), and I'm their only daughter.

It's ironic that their families actually knew each other when Mary & Paul were children in Greece. Paul was from a village in the mountains named Palovaah. Mary was from the sea port, Yithio, a city two miles down the mountainside. During holidays, the villagers would join the city people for celebrations. However, Mary and Paul didn't meet until after they had both separately immigrated to the state of Indiana in the United States of America. What a plot for a movie-of-the-week!

Growing up in an immigrant family was meaningful but not always pleasant. As a young child, I just didn't get it: why did I have to be so different than the other kids on the block? They didn't go to work with their parents. The other children did other things besides just go to Greek functions. Other parents spoke English to their children. And,

2

when I got to school it was even worse. I knew English, yet others were so much better at it. I didn't understand why the other kids spoke better English. Didn't they all come from other countries too?

The Virginia Grill restaurant from the front, at 2512 East Washington Street, Indianapolis, Indiana.
No fancy exterior—simple, straight-forward, and hardworking in appearance, just like most of its crew and customers. (Enlarged details are on following pages.) Paul Vavul and his wife, Mary, lived on the second floor before their daughter was born, after which they moved to a house on North Street and rented out the living space above the restaurant. Five years later they bought the big pink house on a hill, on East 10th Street (near Pleasant Run Parkway).

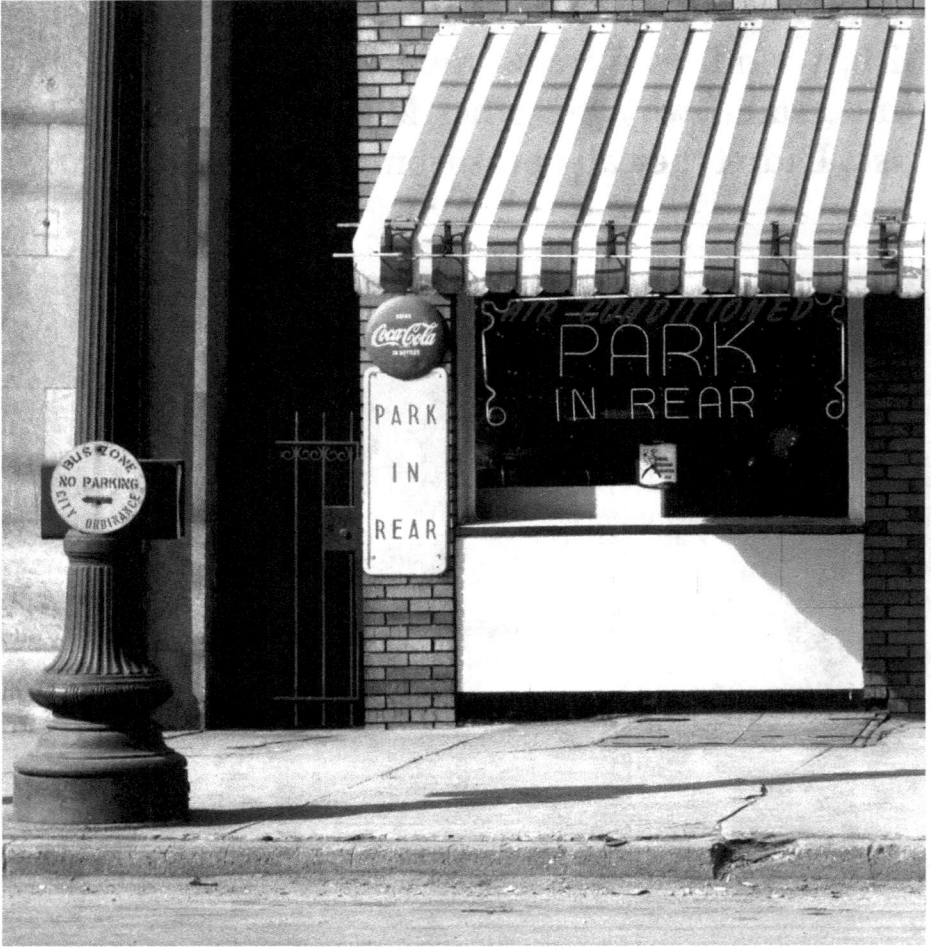

Noticing the details helps us see what life was like in that place and time. There may not at first appear to be anything special in the simple brick building on an imperfect downtown sidewalk, but there was life—both good and bad. Note the iron gate securing the space between buildings, the Coca-Cola sponsored parking sign, the bus zone sign on the styled lamp post, and the notice in the window indicating membership in the Indiana Restaurant Association.

The neon sign across the awning says "PARKING IN REAR." Written on the door is "OPEN 24 hours. Closed Mon." Written across 3 of 5 windows: "Cool," and "Air Conditioned." More signs (neon and hand written) announce services to passers-by: "T-BONE STEAKS," "We Serve BREAKFAST," "CAFETERIA or Table Service," "We Take Orders for PIES to take out."
(Paul Vavul is reflected is in the center window from standing across the street.)

By about the end of first grade I finally began understanding life as a child of immigrants. I began understanding what it meant to be a first-generation "oonited stetes citiyzen."

It meant that I was different than my classmates. My parents had chosen the United States of America. While my classmates and their parents had been here for many generations, my parents were naturalized citizens and I was a new American.

It meant that like anyone in a new land, my mom and dad were more comfortable being around people like themselves. Thus we spoke Greek at home, had only friends who were Greek, and we only went to Greek functions.

I, the first-generation United States citizen was thrown into the world having to learn English, new food, and an entire new culture. And, I was to try teaching my parents the new culture!

It was a huge responsibility for a six or seven-year-old child.

My childhood job of translator was hard, like the day I answered the phone at the grill, only to have the caller ask to speak with someone who "did not have an accent." That hurt. Especially considering that the caller was obviously from a southern state, judging by her accent.

Another time I was charged with explaining to my father the difference between a booth which one sits upon and a boot which goes on your foot.

My mom also came out with some good ones. We never ate broccoli; we ate, and still to this day we eat, broccls.

Another problem was street names. I was almost eleven before I realized that the grill was not on Washington between Tempo and Rule, but was on Washington between Temple and Rural streets.

In every immigrant family there is one over-bearing and prominent rule. Today I call it the "Ethnic Rule." In my own Greek immigrant family, the all-meaning and all-important Ethnic Rule was, "If it is not Greek, it is not good."

My parents did not mean to express themselves so bluntly but Greek is all they knew.

And, no, it does not just apply to Greek families. The Ethnic Rule is shared by any group of people from any country, who among themselves possess a common belief system and culture. They feel that their group, no matter their skin color, is the best and the correct ethnic group.

It is a concept I never understood. I figured that if you bothered to immigrate to another country and be legal in that country, then there must be something good about that country!

To this day, I think about the Ethnic Rule and it still makes no sense to me. However, what does make sense to me is that being in a new country with new people and situations, and not speaking the language of the country, is frightening. Therefore, it was simply more comfortable to be amongst those who were like you. . . . But I still did not like it.

Chapter 2

A Child's Perspective

Even as a young child, I did not accept the Ethnic Rule. In 1960 when I was five, the kitchen was populated with workers who earned a low middle-income wage and who were exclusively African-American. They provided me with the best advice and the best conversations right there in the kitchen of the restaurant.

Cherry was one of those kitchen crew people, who taught me by his somewhat flamboyant nature. He was always in a good mood and he coined the term "Boss Lady" for my mom. Cherry always had on the whitest of aprons and the biggest smile. Cherry was the first homosexual person

I knew. Leave it to the Virginia Grill to teach me that too!

Also in the kitchen crew was Cleo. Cleo was not like the rest of the kitchen crew. He spoke very proper English, and he often came to the house and worked with Dad in the yard. Paul Vavul had a very green thumb. Dad and Cleo were always planting, irrigating or watering. And, they had a constant companion ... St. Spanial (after his death at age fourteen, the family all made Spanial a saint!).

St. Spanial was not just any dog. He followed Paul all around the large and gorgeous yard at any time of the day, but usually at one or two o'clock in the morning, St. Spanial listened to Paul's every word. Spanial responded to everything Paul was saying so appropriately, you'd think they were having a conversation!

Members of the kitchen crew certainly spoke differently than my parents did, and also differently than the nice police officer who came into the Grill at least twice a day. The kitchen crew had a pragmatic way of talking that I could understand.

Irvin, the white-haired and wizened salad and fried chicken man, always told me things so I could understand them. Today, I don't think that his physical appearance was what gave him the talent of explaining things to me—I really think that having seven children of his own had some-

9

thing to do with it.

So I asked Irvin, "What is a rally? And, why is EVERYONE going to it?"

Irvin thought a moment with his chin resting on his hand and then said triumphantly, "The rally is so I can eat at a table in the front of the restaurant, instead of in the kitchen."

Several people in the kitchen mumbled in agreement with Irvin. That sounded like a good reason to me.

So the next day, before Mom and I went to the Grill, I put my fancy red dress and black patent leather shoes into my toy bag, and of course my patent leather purse with the fifteen cents in it. I always took the toy bag to the grill and hung it in the ladies restroom. When it became very busy in the Grill at lunchtime, I snuck into the restroom, changed my clothing and went out the back door to the bus stop.

On the way to the bus stop, I looked at myself in a window and thought, *I look good enough to go downtown.* (My mother always made sure to be well-dressed and wearing gloves and maybe a hat when going downtown, so I felt it was important to be well dressed when I was going downtown.)

The bus would take me to the downtown Circle. The Circle was not just the center of town; it had a big monument that went up to the sky, and a busy street with a lot of cars that went around

10

and around the Circle. Mom and I often took the bus to the Circle when we went shopping, thus I knew exactly what to do.

I had just put my fifteen cents in the fare box of the bus when I heard the voice of Viola (my Mom's housekeeper) yelling, "Miss Tina (short for Stamatina), what are you doing here?!" I calmly explained that I was going to the Rally so that everyone who worked in the kitchen could eat in the dining area like everyone else. I saw a very special smile come across her face (as well as most others on the bus). Viola patted the seat next to her and said, "Here, sit with me." With that pat on the seat I knew I had found a friend and that I was going to the Rally.

When we got to the Circle, Viola handed me off to Cleo, a tall black man I knew from the Grill. Cleo was the person whom my Dad trusted to clean the restaurant's large display of guns twice a year and to work with him in the yard at home. Cleo showed me where all the people were around the Circle. There were people talking on loud-speakers, but honestly, I did not understand what they were saying.

I was very obvious at the Rally. I was the little white face in a sea of dark faces. I could feel that it was something special to be the only white face in a sea of dark faces. People looked at me and smiled. They looked at me with hope in their eyes

11

and faces.

Irvin got me back on the bus which was a good thing, because I did not have another fifteen cents!

Chapter 3

The Kitchen Crew

In the back of the house (the kitchen), along with Cherry and Cleo was the cook, "Booker." Like Cleo, Booker also spoke very proper English. I was told he was from the Indonesian island country of Bali. He taught me how to make the signature Virginia Grill "homemade" noodles.

The noodles were really simple to make. Just put flour, baking soda and a little water together and make a 10"x15"x1/4" flat dough. Cut into 1/4 inch strips. Drag the noodles through loose flour four times, then press the flour into the noodles. Boil the noodles in saltwater. Add the noodles to a side dish round pot, and add the secret ingredient . . . yellow food coloring!

Booker made the noodles every day. There were customers who had noodles with noodles and a side of noodles. One dinner, which several customers ordered was one side of mashed potatoes with two sides of noodles on top!

There were several signs in the restaurant which said, "Taste your food before you season it!" But there were never any signs mentioning calories.

The Grill was managed by two important people. Ollen Gardner was the manager during the day, and at night the manager was Cordie Williams. Let me tell you about these two people.

Ollen got to the Grill theoretically at 8 A.M. I say theoretically because well, sometimes Ollen got a little drunk. In this situation, the police would give dad a courtesy call and Dad would bail him out of the "drunk tank" in the city lockup. Ollen was critical to dad as he was the restaurant's scribe. Therefore, Ollen was the only person for whom Dad would go to the lockup.

Ollen would come in about 8 A.M., and get the menus written for all to see. Then he would make sure that the back of the house, and the front of the house, were ready for the day. Ollen also made sure that Gus, the grill man, was preparing breakfast delicacies like "biscuits and gravy" or "steak and eggs."

13

Photos of opening day.

ABOVE - The proud owner, Paul Vavul is second from the left, and Ollen Gardner, the day manager, is on the far right.

BELOW - Apparently a short break before customers arrive. Normally back then, only white employees would be serving out front.

Items on the menu above their heads include . . .

SANDWICHES: hamburger 25¢, salisbury steak 40¢, pork chop 40¢, chicken 60¢, fish 90¢.
SUGGESTIONS: Jumbo shrimp 6/$1.10, chicken gizzards 6/$1.00, fried oysters 6/$1.25.
BREAKFAST (includes toast & coffee):
2 eggs & sausage 65¢, Chipped beef gravy 50¢, Cereal 20¢, Fruit 15¢ . . . and many other items.

A curious thing happened in my fifth year of working at the restaurant (when I was age ten). My dad decided that I should call Ollen "Mr. Gardner." This is truly a sign of respect for one's elders;

15

however, after five years of referring to him as Ollen, the change was sort of hard to accomplish. So, Mr. Gardner and I had a special "arrangement." Any time I spoke to Mr. Gardner, he knew I meant, "Hey Ollen, please talk to me even though I know who you really are."

Then there was Cordie the night manager. Cordie was a six foot tall woman who hailed from the hills of Kentucky. (No, my father never insisted that I call her Mrs. Williams because this was before the time of women's liberation, which tells you how forceful a woman she was!). Cordie ran the place like a military operation.

At 2 A.M. on Sunday mornings all the bars closed. Then the patrons of the bars came to the Grill for breakfast, and especially for coffee.

In all the years of the Grill I only heard of one time that Cordie lost control. It was one of those after-the-bars-closed-at-2 A.M. periods. Many patrons came from the several bars on Washington Street: the Holyoke Night Club, Blake's, The Ace.

Cordie and the grill man were not getting breakfast out fast enough for some patrons, so the patrons decided that they would help things along by grabbing bread from the cafeteria line and throwing it at Cordie and the grill man. They didn't stop with bread, because the pies were next to the bread. What a mess!

That was the only time I remember a call from

the police asking my Dad to get down to the Grill.

When Dad arrived, he quieted the customers and policemen who were yelling at each other. Then (I am told) Dad made a general announcement to the patrons. I'm sure the patrons did not understand, because he was talking in Greek! However, they understood somehow because the patrons all got quiet and sat in their seats.

Chapter 4

Lasting Impressions

As I mentioned earlier, I liked to be with the kitchen crew and listen to their views on things. Conversations were especially interesting on Fridays. When the mail came on Friday it would contain *The Indianapolis Recorder*—one of the longest published African-American (Black was the appropriate term at that time!) newspaper in the nation.

My Dad would set *The Recorder* on the wall of

his office and it would disappear into the kitchen. Dad always smiled at this event, because he purchased *The Recorder* for the kitchen crew anyway.

In retrospect, the '60s were such a turbulent time—but I didn't know that then. One afternoon, I heard Irvin and some others talking about "the assassination" which was reported in *The Recorder*. No, they were not talking about the assassination of President Kennedy. Rather, they were talking about the assassination of Martin Luther King, Jr. I remember that Thursday evening as if it were yesterday.

It was a Thursday evening, the 4th of April, 1968. I was at the Grill. At roughly 6:30 P.M., we learned that Dr. Martin Luther King, Jr. had been assassinated. There was no TV or radio on out front at the Grill, but Cherry of the kitchen crew always had a radio on. He came to the front of the house and told my Dad. Within ten minutes the entire restaurant knew of the assassination. Mostly a hush came over the Grill. I remember standing near my Mother at the cash register and the whole Grill became eerily quiet.

The Grill was a working man's cafeteria, and at that time there were only white customers and a few rednecks thrown in for diversity's sake. There were customers saying that they were glad MLK was dead.

In my adolescent brain I was furious and horrified that anyone would wish anyone dead! I was also flashing back to a cloudy Friday, when I was in third grade . . .

I remember distinctly my third-grade teacher being called out of the room and exchanging whispers with another faculty member. She then came back in the classroom and did something totally unlike anything she had ever done in the class. She stopped everything, sat on a chair and read us the story of the assassination of Abraham Lincoln. At the close of the story, she put down the book and said to us in a very serious voice, "Something like that has happened to our president today." The class of third-graders was silent, and then there were a few sobs. It was almost time for us to leave. Without being told loudly, and with just a few whispers, all the students went to their buses quickly and quietly.

The assassinations of President Kennedy in 1963, and then Martin Luther King, Jr. in 1968, stand out in my mind as two of those moments in one's life that one will never forget where one was or what one was doing at that moment.

The assassinations were very confusing to me. Two important and well-loved people had been shot and killed by guns. But my dad was a gun collector, and I knew he would never do anything like that. Yet apparently some people would kill other people with guns. Didn't those people realize they were giving guns a bad name? Or did those people who killed other people even care about the gun and how it might be blamed for the assassinations? These questions were too much for my near thirteen year old brain to think about, let alone answer!

Confounding my confusion, on the walls of the Grill was the largest gun collection in the Midwest. And in front of the restaurant was a real cannon, which had been used in World War II. I remember my father having to get a special license for the cannon and for other guns in the collection.

My dad was a gun collector. His collection hung on the walls of the Virginia Grill. People kill other people with guns. It was all so confusing that I was happy (sort of) when the following happened.

Believe it or not, some funny things can happen with guns.

(Inserted on the next few pages are photos of some of Paul Vavul's gun cases which were displayed in the restaurant.)

Paul Vavul had photos of his gun cases made into 8" x 10" black and white prints with his restaurant's name and address at the top.

In this display, the matching pair of large handguns right above the second shelf of bullets (3rd gun from top of case on the left, 4th gun from top on the right), are Remington 1858 revolvers.

The light machine gun out front of the case is a Czech ZB-26. At the left edge of the picture, hanging by a chain, you can see the barrel and magazine of a German MP38 or MP40.

21

The section of this photo copied below has numbers superimposed for the following identifications:

1. Mauser C1896-Broomhandle.
2. Wooden holster/shoulder stock for the C1896.
3. Walther P38

ONE OF TEN GUN DISPLAY CASES AT VIRGINIA GRILL
630 GUNS & RELICS

2512 East Washington St., U. S. Route 40, Indianapolis, Ind.

Vavul had this image printed as full-color postcards.

4. *Ballard rifle.*
5. *Winchester 05/07/10 rifle (model depends on caliber, which can't be known from picture).*
6. *Winchester Model 63.*
7. *Looks like a US Model 1847 Cavalry Musketoon.*

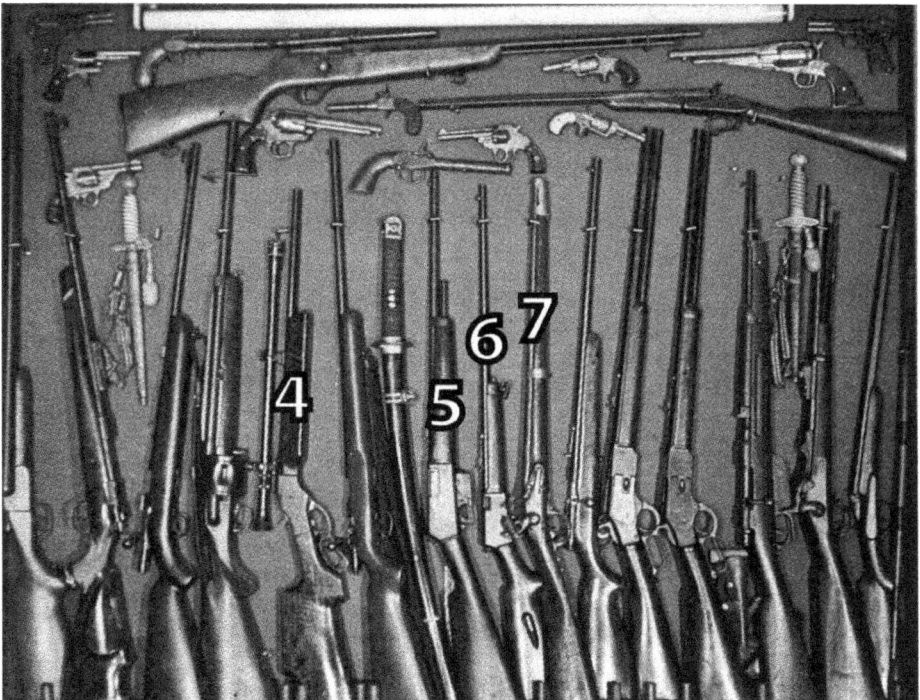

(See next page for identifications)

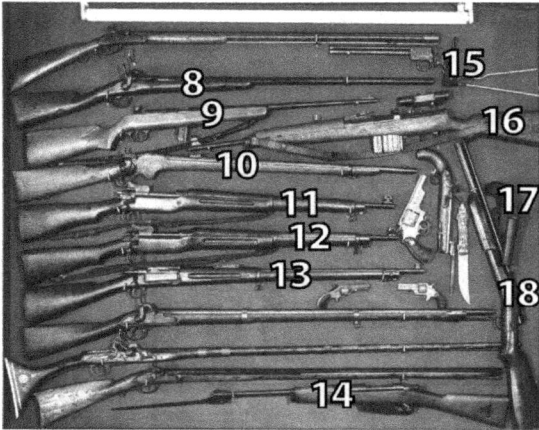

8. Snider Action, probably a shotgun as it has no rear sight and a bead for a front sight.

9. H&R Reising Model 65 .22LR

10. Spencer rifle.

11 & 12. Model 1917 Enfield (could be manufactured by Remington, Winchester or Eddystone).

13. 1898 US Krag rifle.

14. Model 1891 Carcano Carbine.

15. Marble's GameGetter.

16. German G43 Sniper rifle.

17. Flare gun.

18. Air rifle.

19. Winchester model 25 shotgun.

20. Becker revolving shotgun.

21. 98 Mauser sporterized rifle.

22. [Model] 1894 Winchester rifle.

23. [Model] 1894 Winchester Carbine.

24 & 25. 1873 Winchester rifles

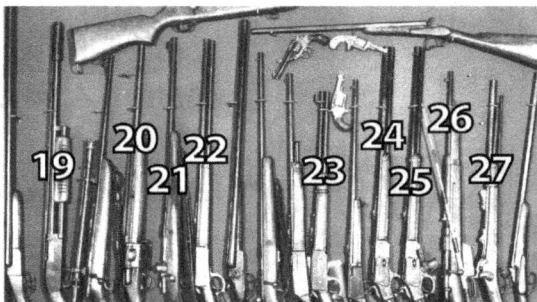

26. 1938 Carcano Carbine

27. 1873 Springfield Trapdoor Cavalry Carbine

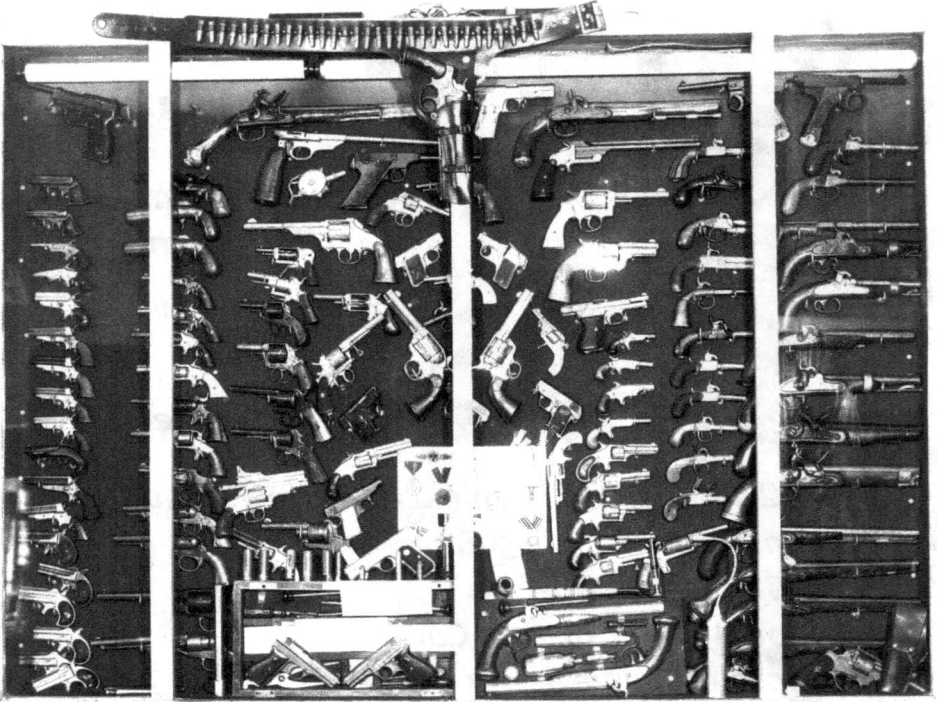

28. Walther P38.
29. Chicago Firearms Co. Protector Palm Pistol.
30. Colt 1903 pistol.
31. Japanese Nambu Type 14.

32. Colt 1873 Single Action Army, Bisley Model.

33. Colt 1873 Single Action Army.

34. 1860 Colt Army.

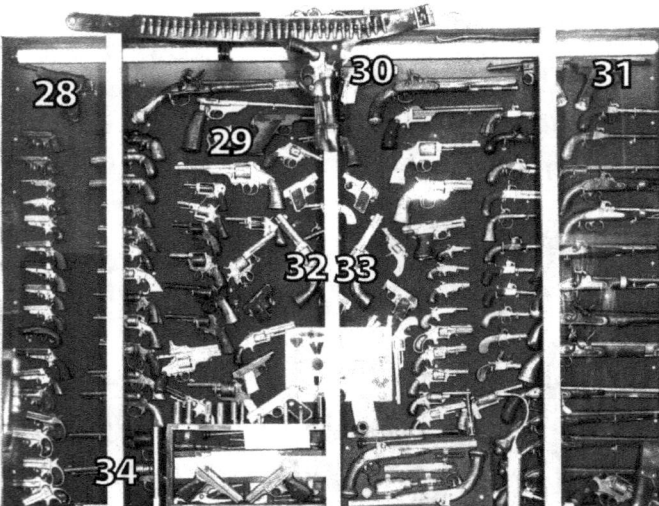

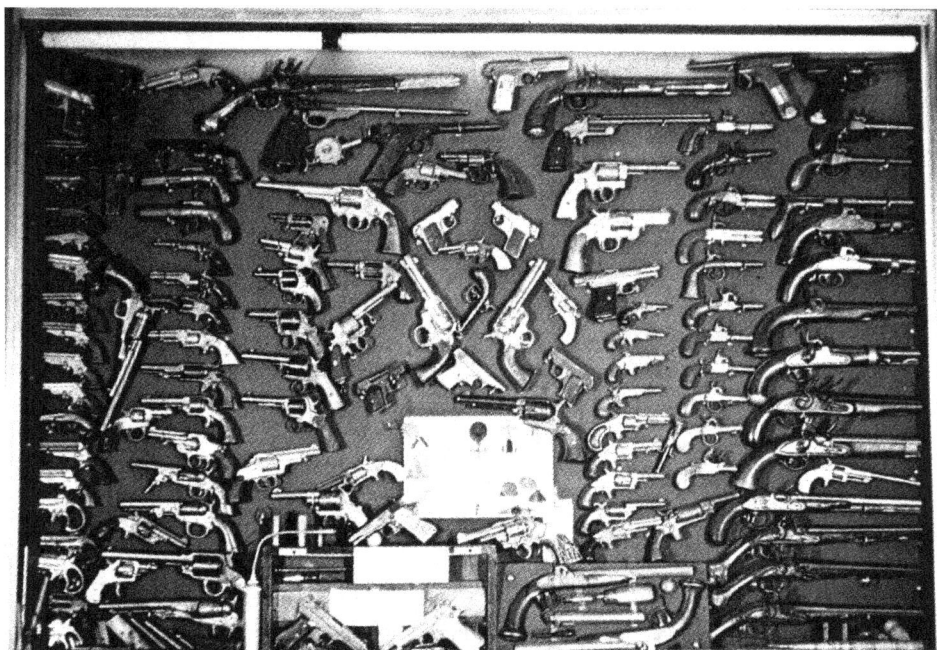

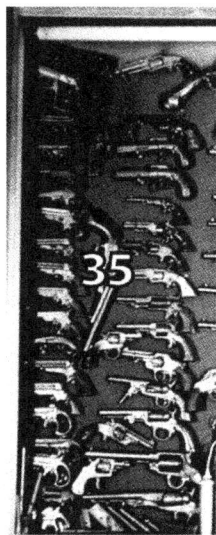

The above photo is of the same display case as previous page, but taken at another time when a few items have been moved and or replaced.

35. Colt 1860 Army with a Richards cartridge conversion.

Chapter 5

Honestly, Occasionally Something Funny Does Happen with Guns

I still smile as I remember the following story. My dad was a licensed covert gun carrier. Actually, he only carried a gun when he went to make a bank deposit. Sometimes he took a surly looking guy from the kitchen with him, but mostly Dad only took his gun—usually stuck in his belt.

Dad used the Fletcher Trust bank (which later became American Fletcher National Bank), which was right next door to the Grill and had a night deposit opening in the front of the bank.

The restaurant was only open until 6 P.M. on Sunday. Then the kitchen crew did heavy duty cleaning. One Sunday night, after making a bank deposit, Dad was driving home on New York Street and the gun fired into his buttocks!

Luckily, my Uncle Ray and family were visiting from Fort Wayne at the time, because my Mom certainly did not know what to do with a gunshot wound! Uncle Ray and the famous Paul Vavul got in the restaurant's highly decorated (guns painted all over it) station wagon, and went to Community Hospital on Rural Street. Uncle Ray went with my dad, because it was thought better that a man should explain the injury rather than my mom (a woman was not to understand or explain such things about a wound in a private area of one's body.)

Dad was fixed up at the hospital, and Uncle Ray and Dad's wounded kolos (Greek for posterior) drove back home to the big pink house at 6601 East 10th Street. By the way, they returned to enjoy the rabbits which had been hunted by Uncle Ray and cooked to perfection by my Mom. Of course, I wouldn't touch the little bunny rabbits for dinner!

This is the only known surviving picture of well-known Virginia Grill station wagon owned by Paul Vavul. Over time, even more gun images were added to the car than can be seen here.

Chapter 6

The Police and the Grill

No, I wouldn't eat the rabbit, but you might be surprised what things did not bother me.

The police and my Dad were good friends. Police often got a free meal, and always free coffee. Their relationship warranted me a few trips with my dad to places most people didn't get to tour.

Once we had to identify people in bloody crime scene photos, and another time we got to see the crime lab. Getting into the lockup or the drunk tank was old hat to me as I went to those locations with my dad on Virginia Grill business on a fairly regular basis.

I don't mean to sound gory; however, that is how it was. Writing this is having more of an effect on me than I thought it would. I feel twelve years old again and my heart is racing as I recite the stories to you fifty-some years after the events. I am using words from my childhood. I would never say "the drunk tank" today, but that is the term I learned as a child.

As I "relive" the stories, I also realize that it wasn't the free coffee that made my dad such good friends with the police. More so it was that Dad was in business in a particular area of the city, and he knew the goings-on and the people of the area. Most importantly to the police though, was that my dad was a very honest person whom they could rely upon.

The police appreciated the generosity of Paul and Mary and the Grill, Especially during 1963 through 1965. Why? Because a few of those "life's moments" which one remembers all through one's life, occurred during those years. There was one disaster after another.

First it was the coliseum explosion on Thursday, October 31, 1963

Halloween was usually a fun time at the Grill. We all got to wear funny clothes, or at least a funny hat. However, October 31st, 1963 will forever be remembered for another Halloween event . . . the Coliseum explosion.

It was the opening night of the *Holiday on Ice* show at the Coliseum. It was a yearly event to which I especially looked forward. I was there with my Mom, her sister and brother-in-law (being my Aunt Helen and Uncle Pete), and my Dad's sister (Aunt Sophie).

I remember sitting on the edge of my seat as the performers were concluding the show. The skating line was going around and around, and at each rotation another performer hurried to catch their place in the line. Visually, it was a very impressive sight to see the performers chasing the line until the whole company was in the line, and the line was skating around the ice.

It was just about 11:00 P.M. All of a sudden my concentration on the performers was shattered by a loud boom. A silence hushed the huge Coliseum as people realized the noise was not part of the show.

The explosion threw many people as much as sixty feet into the air. The performers were the first to realize that something was very wrong and they retreated to the safety of backstage.

The crowd was realizing the seriousness of the situation as mangled bodies landed on the pristine ice and flames shot up where people had been sitting.

My family and I were sitting on the north side of the Coliseum about three rows back from the ice. We were sitting directly across from the area which had blown up.

It wasn't until after we saw the fire that someone yelled "fire!" and everyone started to evacuate the building.

I remember to this day, that in my third grade

class we had just read a book where people were fleeing a disaster, and the book said to remain relaxed and just follow the crowd. That's what I did.

Uncle Pete had driven us to the ice show in the highly decorated Virginia Grill station wagon. As planned, in case anyone got lost, after leaving the building we met at the "wagon."

We were all hugging and crying, when all of a sudden my Mother cried out, "Paul!" All the hugging and kissing stopped as we collectively realized that my Dad, who had let us take the Virginia Grill car so we could all fit, would learn of the disaster, worry about us, and hurry to the Coliseum when he really needed to get down to the Grill to get coffee and sandwiches to the disaster site.

Mom took charge. She hurried everyone into the car and then she took off on foot to learn where the Police had set up their temporary headquarters, and to call Paul.

In about ten minutes, Mom returned saying that the Police let her call Paul on one of their "no wire" phones, and that he would meet us at the Grill. Mom got in the car and started crying again as she said, through her tears, "Paul was so happy to hear from us!"

The second memorable life's event was the assassination of President Kennedy less than a month later.

On Friday, November 22, 1963, I was at Moorhead Elementary School, and I was in third grade. As I said before, I remember distinctly my teacher likening President Kennedy's assassination to the story of Abraham Lincoln's, and all the students going to their buses quickly and quietly.

The quietness continued on the bus, and when I arrived at my stop, I hurried into the house to find my mother sitting by the television with tissues in her hand and reddened eyes, as if she had been crying. We spoke about the events of the day for a moment, and then we got ready to go to the Grill.

When we got to the Grill, again the most appropriate word to explain the ambiance of the Grill was, "quiet." The Jukebox was not layering, and conversations were reserved.

Now, some fifty years later, I realize what instigated the quietness. It didn't matter where one was located (the grill was over 800 miles away from the assassination), we were part of a nation mourning the loss of its President, and that grief was expressed through quietness.

The third sad event was the discovery of Miss Likens.

A couple of years had passed since JFK, and everyone was doing well. The Grill had returned to its regular noisy self. The highly decorated Virginia Grill station wagon, and Paul himself, had not been at a disaster scene for almost two years.

Then, when we thought that nothing else would or could happen . . .

It was a Tuesday evening at the Grill (October 26, 1965), about 7 P.M. when we heard a siren. In itself that was not unusual—we were on a very busy street. However, then there were three sirens, then more than one could count! The sirens alerted us that something serious was happening nearby. In a house a few blocks away, a sixteen-year-old girl named Sylvia Marie Likens had been discovered tortured to death.

The Virginia Grill made sure that all the police and other professionals had food and lots and lots of coffee for the long and emotionally difficult investigation.

I for one was glad when the media eventually began concentrating on other events. I wanted to respect Ms. Likens, yet just didn't want to hear every little detail again and again.

Chapter 7

About Paul

Did you know that my Dad could not read or write well in Greek or in English? We called his writing "Greeklish." In other words, part English letters, part Greek! But he managed to live life to the fullest. He was a great problem solver. For example, let me tell you about rubber stamps and "The Suits."

"Rubber Stamps"

As far as reading and writing goes, I suspect Paul Vavul was a strong visual learner. He knew what his name looked like. As a matter of fact, that is also how he paid household bills—by knowing what things looked like.

In the basement of our house, was a desk with a rubber stamp tree. On each rubber stamp was a picture and some "Greeklish" indicating what the stamp said.

Also on the desk was a check writing machine. The user had to put the numbers into the machine, and it would print out the numbers in words on the check.

Unfortunately, these techniques would not work at the Grill. There was just too much writing to be done. However, the suits helped circumvent this problem.

"The Suits"

In April of 1962 two men in black suits cornered Mr. Vavul and wanted to see "the books" for the restaurant. They showed him their fancy badges (which he gave to me to inspect . . . they looked real; what did I know besides how to read and write English?).

So Paul honestly said to them, "What books?"

One of the men in the black suits said, "The books for the store. How do you know if you made any money if you do not keep books?"

Paul Vavul smiled and said, "It's simple! I pay all the bills cash out of the drawer including payroll. If there is money in the drawer at the end of the week, I made money!!" The "suits" were definitely not used to working with people from the "old country"!

After the "Suits," Dad hired Uncle Pete to do the books. And by "hired," I mean that loosely—I think Uncle Pete did the books so he and Aunt Helen could have dinner at the Grill every night!

The big change after the "Suits" had to do with hours. Since its opening, the grill had been open 24 hours every day. After the "Suits," the Grill was closed every Sunday night at 6 P.M. until Tuesday at 5 A.M. Not only did this give everyone a break, it also kept the Grill from elevating to the next tax bracket.

"Aha" you say. You think Dad had Uncle Pete do his household writing too? No. He continued to use the rubber stamps and check writing machine! They were a way he could be independent and "the man of the house."

ABOVE: *Front of Charga-Plate*
BELOW: *Back of Charga-Plate*

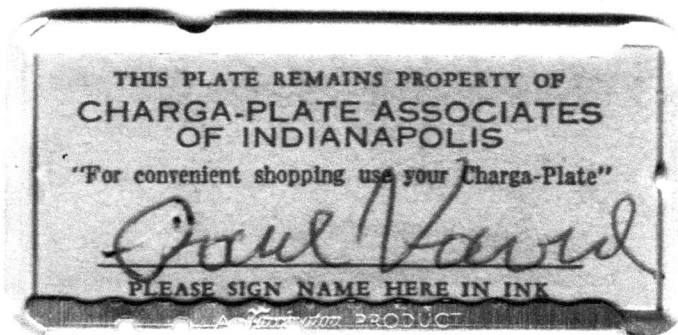

The "Charga-Plate" was another item which facilitated business; it was an early version of the credit card. Vavul's name and address embossed on the metal card could be impressed on a paper record of each purchase to be billed to Vavul. The notches on the edges indicated at which stores Vavul had authorized charge accounts.

PREVIOUS PAGE: Leather cover for the Charga-Plate.

Chapter 8

More About Paul

Paul Vavul was very concerned that his restaurant, the Virginia Grill, always had at least a 98% rating from the health department. He thought any lesser rating would give the independent restaurant a bad reputation.

Twice a year, a health inspector would come into the Grill and ask for Mr. Vavul. Everyone who worked at the grill knew that if someone asked for Mr. Vavul, it would probably be the health inspector. Word about the visit would quickly and quietly filter through the front of the house and into the back of the house. It was the only time I ever saw Mr. Vavul take his time reaching someone. Not that there was anything wrong at the grill; it was just that Dad didn't like "big brother" looking in on his business.

Inevitably, the inspector would make notes on his thick pad of forms, as he went through the entire restaurant. Sometimes he even went down into the cellar, which was only used to store bottled drinks. One time when the inspector entered the walk-in refrigerator, he noted on his pad of papers that the special Rubbermaid container which was filled with the ends of all kinds of breads did not have a very secure lid.

The inspector always made his way to the very back—the out building behind the restaurant which housed several deep freezers. I remember thinking that it was a good thing that the inspector did not go into the freezer that had Dad's eleven inch long frozen goldfish, which he was going to take to the taxidermist—*some* time.

And then there's the story of becoming a Mason...

One year, Paul got it in his mind that he wanted to be a 32nd degree Mason.

I don't understand all the Lodge designations, but it was important to him. I started seeing his friend Bob at the grill a lot. Sometimes Bob brought his wife, Annette, to the grill too. Bob and Annette became great friends with Paul and Mary and were often invited to the house too. Then I noticed books about Masonry on dad's desk at home and at the Grill. I finally figured it out: dad was studying to be a 32nd degree Mason and Bob was helping him.

I could not imagine a man who was illiterate,

in both Greek and English, learning the requirements of the 32nd degree Mason. Why was I so surprised though? We are talking about the man who was the Treasurer of the Greek Orthodox Church at one time too.

Paul Vavul did become a member of the Masonic Lodge. He was very dedicated and proud to act as stage manager for their rituals.

Mary Kargakos, 1953 (the year before marrying Paul).

Chapter 9

"Behind Every Great Man
is a Great Woman" . . .

. . . Is how the saying goes. How true that was in the case of my parents.

When Mary (my Mom) first came to this country, she worked for her Uncle Peter in Ft. Wayne, Indiana. The family was in the theater business. She did not have a glamorous job, yet it was an important job—running the concessions. Because most of her job included popcorn, her name became "Mary Mary, popcorn Mary. She did have a sense of humor though. Anytime someone called her by this little rhyme, she had a smile on her face.

Mary married Paul in 1954 and became an active worker at the restaurant. Though she was not one of the managers, she certainly had a "presence" at the Grill. As a matter of fact, all the staff fondly called her "Boss Lady." Mostly she operated the cash register. She was also in charge of employees who sometimes needed a little help.

One night after Mom and I had worked at the Grill, we took home with us a very frightened girl from somewhere in South America. She had been brought over by someone who promised her a job and a "green card." Whoever "they" were, they got her a "green card" (which was probably not a legal green card) and literally dropped her off at the Grill. Having seen this situation before, Dad gave her a job and mom took her with us when we went home.

When we drove into the driveway of 6601 E. 10th Street, she exclaimed how beautiful was the big pink house on a hill. As a smart aleck nine year old, I said, "And that's where you are going to stay tonight!" To which she exclaimed, "Oh no. I couldn't!" To which my Mother exclaimed, "Yes you can and yes, you will. You are in America now. You know, we all came from somewhere!"

Another person helped by my mom and dad was a man who had taken the name Americanos (Greek for one who is American). Dad took him under his wing and to the house numerous times on Sundays after church. He and dad had a good time talking and watching war movies.

Yes, war movies! When Dad came back from World War II, the ship he was on had a lot of war movie footage that the State Department wanted destroyed. Dad somehow got a hold of the footage and managed to get it back to the states. Dad and friends would spend hours in the basement of the house on 10th Street watching the footage on a 16mm projector. Some of the footage has been donated to the Indiana Film Archive.

It was quite common for immigrants to help other immigrants. Both Mom and Dad felt that since they were so fortunate in the United States of America, it was their responsibility to help immigrants from any country. However, my favorite story was how Mom and Dad helped a man from Greece named Jimmy.

Jimmy was a 35-ish year old man who had a family "back home." He lived in a room in a house in the neighborhood. He worked as a busboy for six months, one or two shifts a day. Then he went "home" for a month, and returned to repeat the entire procedure.

Eventually, Jimmy became a citizen and brought his family to the States. The family of six moved to Chicago where Jimmy was employed in another restaurant. The entire process took nearly ten years. I must tell you a funny story about Jimmy . . .

The restaurant closed at 6 P.M. on Sunday night until 5 A.M. on Tuesday morning. I noticed that Jimmy always ate a very large meal at the restaurant on Sunday evening (employees were allowed one free meal a day at the Grill).

Kiddingly, one Sunday night I asked Jimmy (in Greek of course) if he was going to eat tomorrow.

He answered me in Greek, "Of course not. The restaurant is closed on Monday so I will not eat until it opens on Tuesday!"

...I don't think I have ever met a harder working more spendthrift man than Jimmy.

Several times I have mentioned that Mom and Dad had a great sense of humor. Following is a classic Mom story.

The grill often provided food for special occasions. We did box lunches for the 500 mile race, and box dinners for the 500 mile race parade. One time in the mid-'60s, Zeko—the then Gypsy King—passed on, and the Virginia Grill did all the food for three days.

There were several thousand Romany camped out at or near the Dorsey funeral home on New York Street. One person representing all of the Romany people at the funeral, paid the funeral home for services and damages, and did the same to the Virginia Grill.

Sometime after the funeral, Mom tore a rotator cuff muscle in her shoulder. She was in Community Hospital on Rural Street. It was a very painful and serious operation, and required her to have a hard cast on her arm with her arm in traction

46

pointing straight up to the ceiling.

There was a hospital administrator in charge of making sure visitors were gone by 8:00 P.M. My mom was loved by many people and had many well-dressed visitors. At 8:42 P.M., the administrator could no longer stand having visitors on the floor.

The administrator came into Mom's room and explained, loudly, that visitors must leave!

Mom, with a stern straight face, looked at the administrator and said, "My dear, don't you realize I am not a regular patient? I am the Gypsy queen!"

Chapter 10

May in Indianapolis

The month of May in Indianapolis was always a good time. The Virginia Grill often served as a meeting place, or a starting and ending place, for May activities. When I was in my early teens, my cousins from Ft. Wayne would come to Indianapolis—not for the big race in May, but for the activities we planned race weekend.

The seven of us would breakfast at the grill, and then take the bus downtown to the Circle and visit our first stop, the Indianapolis Power and Light Company building. Why was this so exciting? Because we liked to watch the big panel of thirty-six colored lights which changed each time the elevator stopped at a different floor. There was a sign outside that said "No Loitering. No Solicitation." but I figured that since I owned stock in the company (all twelve shares of it) we could go in and watch the pretty elevator lights.

Our next stop would be the L.S. Ayres department store. Each of us made important purchases. One cousin and I had to have the latest in cosmetics— fake finger nails which were sold in a box and which you glued on (and they looked atrocious). Another cousin needed the latest Beatles album, and one or two cousins we parked in the book department until we retrieved them when we were ready to head back to the grill.

With all our purchases in hand, there was one last stop at Morrow's Nut House on the Circle to get snacks before catching the bus back to the Grill. Back at the Grill we had to listen to my Mother's chastisement concerning our ridiculous purchases.

But really, how bad were we? We didn't use drugs, we didn't wreak havoc, we never skipped school, we never even smoked cigarettes, and we would never have touched a gun! Compared to today's society, we were angels!

So what's behind the change? Why are so many of today's kids less angelic, and why have there been so many shootings in recent years?

Sit back and think with me . . .

Let's reminisce together. Do you member that when we were kids we valued life? Many of us would not/will not hurt a fly. (Okay, except maybe the fly that was crawling on your birthday cake.)

Fifty years ago (yes, I remember that far back), did we see people killed in movies, and on television? Sure we did. Yet killing was not in high-definition color, and not glamorized and thought of as being "routine." We were not desensitized to killing.

Here's another thing. Remember when one could walk into a store and hear calming "elevator music"? It is no secret that retailers know what type of music makes the consumer relax and spend money. However, today's society no longer reacts to elevator music. Today's consumer is motivated by loud music with a strong, consistent and loud rhythm. Watch people in any Wal-Mart. You will probably see children and even some adults acting like what they hear in their environment—loud raucous noise.

The above areas are currently being researched by many people. One area however, which is different than the above, and which has not been researched thoroughly, is "values."

In order to talk about values, we must first define that term "value."

A value is something which is not tangible, yet it is a concept or belief that each person feels so strongly about that each person lives by their values—whether they know it or not. In other words, values are a visceral part of each person.

People are not born with values. Values are learned from one's parents and/or environment. A person can also be influenced to delete and replace their values.

Now that we have established a rudimentary definition of values, let us return to the question "why have there been so many shootings in recent years?" No, it's not just that guns and accoutrements are readily available. Actually, guns were even *more* available fifty years ago.

It could be that some of the recent indiscriminate killing is attributable to mental illness, but what would be behind increased cases of mental illness, or behind those which are not so attributable?

Could it be that too many people are not thoughtfully and consciously choosing the values they live by?

I encourage parents to discuss values with their children. Don't leave it for the school; the school has enough to do and will often say values are too much like religion.

Don't leave the "values" discussion for your religion to teach to your children; religions are the biggest culprit in confusing values and religion. Religions tend to teach values as part of the religion. That is fine. However, values can be separate from religion too.

Most importantly, don't leave the values discussion to your child's peers; peers do not know any more about values than your own child. Peers often confuse what they see and hear in their environment as the values they should accept.

In other words, if you want your child to be reliant on others, and (usually) full of misinformation, let them learn values haphazardly. If you want your child to grow to be an independent thinking human being, be sure to foster values in your child by discussing them and giving reasons for each value you feel is important and appropriate.

I'm sure many of you are saying, "So, what are your values?"

Following is a description of some of my values which support each of my personal goals.

VALUES — Living and health, as well as knowledge, wisdom, and intellectual status.
GOAL — I will do my best to live to 120 in *good shape!*

VALUES — Individual rights, responsibility, integrity, leadership, caring, family happiness.
GOAL — To manage my life and help others manage their own lives.

VALUE — Spirituality.
GOAL —To understand life and death and maybe come around for another life too!

So what are your values? The above lists what I value, but there are many other values you could choose. Look on the net or devise your own words, but make sure they describe ideas you believe in and live by.

I did study and receive a Ph.D. in Counseling (psychology), but I think the major factor in my intellectual path was all the people of the Virginia Grill.

Back to the Grill . . .

When all the cousins became junior or senior

high school age we decided it was time to experi-
ence the Indy 500 Mile Race. So, we did our downtown tour the day before, then everyone had breakfast at the grill, and everyone then marched to
Uncle Pete's car. Uncle Pete usually got volun-
teered for this type of activity.

As we all clambered into the car, someone
handed Uncle Pete a box full of delicious hot Virginia Grill-made donuts. He briefly put the box on
top of the car to get out his car keys, and then he
got into the car and we drove off. It took not even
a mile for everyone to realize that something had
fallen into the street from the roof of Uncle Pete's
car. So much for those hot delicious donuts.

*(Citations and references have been
omitted from the above chapter in order
to make reading easier.)*

Chapter 11

Marketing Marketing Marketing!

Paul knew how to market the Grill and get people to dine at the Grill time and time again. How did he accomplish this? Paul Vavul had a few memorable tools.

In about December of 1960 (I was probably in the 1st grade), I remember going to my station behind the salads and breads and finding many calendars on top of the salad and bread display shelves. I remember saying to myself that they were a good idea, because they all touted the Virginia Grill and were free for the taking!

The next year I found many boxes in dad's office, which each contained a scissor and letter opener set. Occasionally, I will see one of these sets in someone's home or office to this day.

However, nothing beats the year he gave out Virginia Grill bottle openers! To this day, if you knew of the Virginia Grill in the most cursory manner, you are likely to have seen a white bottle opener with a red cap and fringe on it, which touts the Virginia Grill. I don't know how they got worldwide; I saw them in France, England and in Israel! I've had reports of them being in Japan and Taiwan.

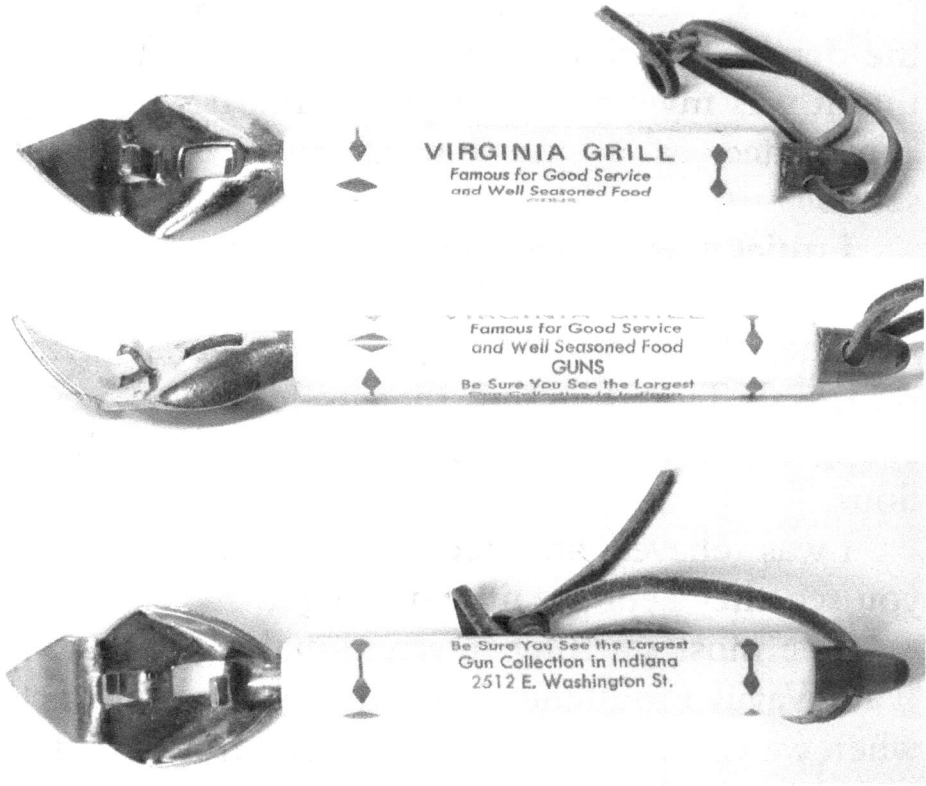

Neat looking and useful, many of these bottle/can openers were printed with red ink and red-tipped handles, touting Virginia Grill's well seasoned food and "largest gun collection in Indiana."

A special gift he gave out any time of the year was a little miniature derringer cigarette lighter. They were almost as coveted as the bottle opener. I really liked this tool. They were really cute. They also got me in big trouble.

I was in fourth grade and heard my name being called to the principal's office at Moorhead Elementary School on E. 10th Street. I entered the principal's office with a big smile as I saw one of the derringer lighters on his desk. Then I found that it was my derringer lighter! And it was being confiscated as a gun having been brought to school!

I quickly explained that it was a make-believe gun, and it was really a lighter.

Then I saw the principal talking to the vice principal. They told me that as long as I never brought this to school again, no harm had been done.

I was relieved, and peeved at the same time-you see, they kept my little derringer!

The most startling international sighting of a "Paul Vavul Production" was in a restaurant once when we visited London. I looked up from my fish and chips, grabbed my father's arm, and pointed to the TV on the wall. It was showing a picture of our house on 10th Street in Indianapolis, which was decorated with Christmas lights.

Actually, I am putting it mildly. Every year,

from December 1st through January 2nd, Dad put up thousands of lights and many fiberglass creatures. My favorite was always the big Rudolph with the flashing red nose. People would drive miles and miles to see the display. The display used so much electricity that Indianapolis Power and Light Company put up an extra transformer for the display, so that it would not cause a blackout in the area. There was also plenty of music on the loudspeakers at our house, and often someone (usually me) handing out candy canes to each car full of visitors.

Here are a few of the many Christmas decorations at the Vavul home, which gained Paul Vavul a lot of attention. He installed more lights and decorations in the years following this photo.

I want to explain something here, for any acquaintances of my parents or myself who may be reading this: my parents were Greek Orthodox Christians. I am not. Here, briefly, is how that happened . . .

In Sunday school one morning, the priest came in to explain the Trinity to the Sunday School children. One little first grader raised her hand and asked, "So, who is God?" The priest never answered the child but shook his head making a comment like "Someday you'll get it maybe." In other words, he paid no attention to the child. (That was just one particular priest. I actually liked most of the Eastern Orthodox priests.) The child then went on a quest to find a belief system which met her convictions.

I must admit, I was exposed to different belief systems at an early age. And yes, the Grill did this too! To many of the kitchen crew, Jesus was part of the Godhead, the Trinity. The man from Iran, who sold the Grill tea, was a rare Coptic Christian. Occasionally, a Muslim patron would come in, and people of many other belief systems. I spoke with them about their religion and lifestyle.

Remember how the Ethnic Rule made no sense to me? Neither did the religion in which I had been raised. I really felt and still feel that God is not corporeal, but that there is a little bit of God in everyone, and all the bits of God together form that spirit which is colloquially known as God.

I continued studying belief systems, and in order to follow my convictions, I settled on, and converted to, Judaism in 1974—at the age of 18.

More Vavul marketing—custom printed matchbooks.

Chapter 12

Days in the Life . . .

Dad did not arrive at the Grill until 10 A.M., and he always stayed through the dinner rush. He usually got home from the Grill about 10 P.M., and then he relaxed with friends, family, and his B&L (Bond and Lillard whiskey).

He had a very specific way of making a drink for himself. He put ice in a glass, poured over it a couple of shots of the B&L, and then took the glass in both hands and whispered the next ingredient over the top of the glass . . . "Water." A smile often accompanied the utterance of "water."

Dad was not a Saint when it came to whiskey. He had his "B&L" with him in his one person office every night. Yet, he did not stay out past 10 P.M.

Many times I could go a week without seeing him at home, because I was already asleep when he came home. Sometimes though, he came home on a Friday night a little early, and we would have a "peanut party."

A "peanut party" involved him and me sitting in the family room with mixed nuts, beer nuts, and hard, salted garbanzo nuts, and watching Sammy Terry on the scary late show.

I may ring some alarms about my dad's drinking, however that is the way it was, and it helped me meet my future father-in-law. Across Washington Street and down a bit, was Dad's favorite drinking buddy—George Samson of Samson Paper Company. Not only were they drinking buddies, but they were also very ecumenical.

You see, old man Samson would hit up old man Vavul for a donation to the Jewish National Fund, and old man Vavul would hit up old man Samson for a donation to the Greek Church. Of course, each donation was consummated with hundred year old, Old Grand Dad whiskey.

Paul Vavul did have a son, who was much older than me and not living at home most of my life. However, he also had a god-son, Stan, with whom Dad was very close. Stan would come down from Fort Wayne during summers and work at the Grill.

While researching this book I spoke to Stan (whom I always considered a cousin), and he told me how he started out as a dishwasher, was promoted to a bus boy, and finally made it to the serving of vegetables on the cafeteria line. He said he was always sad that he never made it to number one—serving entrées.

Behind the cash register, above single-serving boxes of breakfast cereals (Wheaties, Kellogg's Corn Flakes, Bran Flakes, Grape Nuts, and Rice Krispies), hung these photos. The man is Paul Vavul, in his Army uniform. When the army found out during basic training that he could cook, they sent him to cook in North Africa. Before marrying Mary Kargakos, Paul and his first wife had adopted a son, Stephen, who is the boy on the left. When that marriage dissolved in the early 1950s, Paul got custody of Stephen—which is a sign of Paul's outstanding character.

Stan told me stories about my Dad which I had never heard. I always thought that Dad never, ever drew his gun, but Stan told me my Dad did draw a gun on someone once. Stan recited the story to me . . .

Mom was, as usual, at the register. A tall, mean looking guy approached her pointing a gun at her and demanding money. Little did the thief know that Dad was in his little office, until Dad stood up and exclaimed, "You expletive expletive" (in Greek of course), "there is a gun pointed right at you, and if you leave right now no one will know about this."

The gunman put his gun down on the counter and hurried out the front door!

Mom was rather shaken up, so Dad put his arm around her and comforted her.

Mom said of the gun (in her humorous way of yelling in Greek in a high and very loud voice, and with the gun still pointing at her), "Paul, get that thing out of here!"

Stan said that when he was fourteen years old, it wasn't unusual for my Dad to tell him to get into the highly decorated Virginia Grill station wagon, saying, "Come on, we're going somewhere." Obediently, Stan would do so.

During one particular trip, Paul Vavul was uncomfortably somber, while my cousin was his usual funny self. The wagon stopped in the parking lot of the Dorsey Funeral Home. Stan was a little surprised yet followed my dad like a puppy, wherever he went.

I was surprised to hear from Stan that the ride back to the grill, while still somber, contained some interesting dialogue . . .

Paul Vavul had said to Stan, "I'm glad you went with me. It really helped that you came with me.

You really helped, because this was a very hard thing to do."

When Stan told me the story, it hit me: I knew that Dad's best friend had passed away one summer, but I did not know that it was Stan who went with Dad to the viewing.

Stan also had a revelation: "Oh, so that is why he was so somber!"

Chapter 13

Finding Solace in the Neighborhood

Some people use religion in which to find solace. Not me. From my earliest days at the Grill, the Brown Library was my place of comfort . . . and horse stories. I have no idea why I was so drawn to horses. However, my fascination with horses has never ended. My husband and I attend several horse shows each year.

On our way to the Grill, Mom would often drop me off at the Brown Library.

The library was located in an old large house. One trudged up a flight of stairs, to reach the front door. I always thought that the staircase should have been guarded by lionesses. Why female lions? Because I thought that female lions would be more protective of the many children who used the library.

Once at the front door, you were confronted by the librarian's stand. They always whispered a quiet "hello."

Then, if you really wanted to look up something, you went to the left around the stand. I always turned to the right and headed straight for the books about horses.

I said I don't know where I got this fascination with horses and everything about horses, which lasts yet today; but on second thought, I do realize why the library and horses were so important to me—because everything I did was for my parents, except horses and the library were something my parents could not do. Horses and the library were truly the first things I ever did just for myself.

Walter Farley, Anna Sewell, Alois Podhajsky, and Marguerite Henry (authors of horse books) were important people in my young life, and I spent countless hours with them. Sometimes I would gallop like a horse, the four blocks back to the Grill. You can be sure I was holding tightly to some of my "friends" (books) on the way.

Chapter 14

My First Uniform

As a small child I usually wore slacks and a nice shirt with an apron over them. Then, one day, when I was about seven or eight my dad proclaimed to my mother that she should get me a uniform. I was thrilled! I was taller than anyone else in my second grade class, and I hated working in a shirt and slacks even though the apron covered me to the floor.

So off to the uniform shop mom and I went.

I was flipping through the uniforms on a rack when my mother came over to me and said that those uniforms were too "old" for me. Her comment didn't make too much sense to me, but I did what I was told like a good girl.

I looked through the rack, which was approved by my mother, and she picked out a uniform and told me it was the right one for me. Surprisingly, I actually liked it. It was plain white with fancy buttons on the front and a round neck.

I mention this type of shopping, because this was the only way we ever shopped. She told me, what was right for me. This ethnic way of shopping lasted until high school. Then I became old enough to know what was right for me.

I am not complaining about the ethnic way of shopping . . . well, yes I am! There was very little freedom or independent thinking in our ethnic household. I was told that little girls were to be seen and not heard. It was a difficult upbringing because I insisted on doing something that my parents hated: I thought for myself at a very early age.

As I got older, my mother learned that I could make good decisions, and by so doing I could save her a lot of time and energy. And, of course, my going shopping by myself was fine with me.

It was not unusual to see me as a well-dressed thirteen-year-old in a hat and gloves taking the bus downtown. Mostly when I went on shopping expeditions, I went because I needed a particular item like when September came around, and I had no clothing for school.

Yes, mom told me what to get as it had to fit her specifications. For example, when short skirts were the fashion in the '60s, no, my skirts had to go down past the knee. In order to meet Mom's specifications, I ended up in an older women's section, where I had no interest in being; but that was the only place I could find skirts over the knee. Even though Mom came from a long line of seamstresses, she never realized that fashions change.

When I was in ninth grade my father needed to get out of the Grill for a while. He just needed a break, so my mom sent us on a trip to England, Scotland and Ireland. Little did I realize that fashion on the other side of the pond was extremely different.

I head finally gotten her to allow me some paisley bell-bottoms. I was so proud of those slacks. They were the "in thing" and looked great on me. However, little did I know that they were not the rage in England, Scotland or Ireland. I got cat calls any time I wore them! Was it because of the slacks, or because I was walking with an obviously older-than-me man? I will never know, but I did not wear the slacks again till I was back in the states.

Chapter 15

What Happened to the Guns?

The Grill was sold upon my father's retirement in 1970, but the guns did not go with the sale. Instead, my parents did a really smart thing—they spent the early years of their retirement traveling around the country to gun shows, selling the collection a piece at a time.

In the 1970s, gun shows did not require extensive background checks and were considered reputable. It was a great way to travel the country and live off the sale of the collection.

I was a sophomore in high school when they started traveling. My Aunt, who already lived with us, stayed home with me while Paul and Mary traveled.

Every Wednesday was the same. My aunt and I watched as the big white Cadillac's trunk was open while Paul Vavul loaded his precious collection.

Each gun was wrapped in a towel and placed in the trunk of the car. As the trunk got more and more full of guns, the rear end of the car got lower and lower. When the collection was loaded and the car was close to the ground, mom and dad and that Cadillac looked like they were doing something illegal, and "getting out of town."

The out-of-town part was correct. They traveled to Texas, and visited a restaurant where no one was allowed to wear a tie. Therefore, one of the treasures Mary and Paul brought back was a tie cut in half.

They went to California, Arizona, and Missouri. They even visited me at College in Milwaukee, Wisconsin, where I attended a gun show with them. It was held in a large Convention Center hotel on the south side of the city.

There were rows and rows of eight foot tables loaded with guns and weapons of all kinds. Some people were selling military and accoutrements like patches, pins, knives and mortar shells.

None of the guns were loaded, and proper gun etiquette was strictly followed. In other words, if one held up a gun to look through a scope, even though it was not loaded, it would not be pointed at anyone.

I really liked the values shown at gun shows in the '70s. People were considerate and deals were sealed with a handshake. Yes, yes, there was paperwork to be done too, but after the handshake you could wait a while to do the paperwork. People were friendly to each other at the gun shows. They often saw each other at various shows, and would join each other for dinner or general socializing.

On their last trip to Arizona, mom and dad and the guns were involved in an accident. Everyone was fine except for the big white Cadillac.

On a Thursday evening, we got a call from Mom and Dad saying that they would be home in two hours. Excitedly, my aunt and I cleaned up the house, and awaited their arrival. Sure enough, within the two hour time frame they drove into the their driveway in a . . . green Cadillac! We did not recognize them at first, because they had always driven a white Cadillac—until that accident in Arizona.

Chapter 16

The Tour

Pardon me! All this talk about the Grill, and I have not yet taken you on a tour!

When one came in the front door of the Virginia Grill, he or she walked into a breezeway and then opened another door to the Grill itself. A quick right turn and you were by the trays and cutlery and napkins. Then you faced "the line."

The line began with the steam table and entrées: first slot would always be fried chicken neighbored by a special-of-the-day (often roast round of beef). Other specials-of-the-day could be Swiss steak, baked cod, or ham hock's and sauerkraut.

Then, one's eyes and nose noticed the vegetables or side dishes. This is where one could order the famous Virginia Grill, homemade noodles. More common side dishes included mashed potatoes, green beans, kale, beans or corn. Even the corn was special—it had little red things in it. I knew not what they were, but they tasted good.

Next on the line were salads and the bread department. With every meal went an order of either hot rolls, Vienna, rye, white or wheat bread, and a salad of your choice or two vegetables. Then the fun started . . . deserts.

There were always two seasonal cobblers and then the case of pies. There were chocolate pies, banana cream, lemon, apple, blueberry, and custard . . . in other words, whatever the patron wanted.

There was a blank space next, where a friendly person (often me) asked and retrieved the patrons drink order. Popular choices were coffee (which was located directly behind the drink person), or (in order of what was served most), Coca-Cola and Pepsi, 7-Up, and Root Beer. These soft drinks were in back of the drink person and to their right, in a refrigerated "cooler" which also contained milk, skim milk, buttermilk and chocolate milk. Beer was another popular drink. The Grill sold a lot of Budweiser, followed by Pabst Blue Ribbon, and Miller. We also had Michelob, and Wiedemann.

At the end of the line during lunch and dinner rushes, was the best marketing tool of all. Paul Vavul would place a fresh glass of water on each patron's tray and offer a hello or small talk.

One got to the back of the house by going through a swinging door with a window in it. On the left was where the dishwasher person scraped food into a big waste container. Then the dishwasher person would rinse the dishes with a spray head of water and put them into the dishwasher itself. Further back in the kitchen were stovetops, ovens, and work tables.

Then there was one of my favorite places—the walk in refrigerator. On the shelves were trays of food ready to be warmed and put on the steam table. Next was all kinds of fresh vegetables and my favorite Rubbermaid container full of the heels of all kinds of bread.

There was another unattached building which housed freezers. I rarely had to go to that building. So, the big container of stale bread remains my favorite area of the walk in refrigerator. Probably it was my favorite because the next time I saw the same pieces of stale bread, they had become bread pudding.

I learned many things from the restaurant and my parents. America is a wonderful place, and one can live the New American Dream, but only if he or she works at it. I learned last, that hard work makes you feel good about yourself and your surroundings, and to never give up. In other words, the most important lesson from the Grill is . . . "With stale bread, you make bread pudding."

On opening day, the Grill was filled with bouquets!
ABOVE: Life Savers candy sits by the cash register.
BELOW: "The line" full of tasty foods.

More photos of opening day.
ABOVE: You can see the Jukebox on the right.
BELOW: The gun display case shown on the cover of this book, is at the far end of the room.

Quite a bit roomier with-out the flowers.

The sign over Paul's head says, "Get your souvenir from Virginia Grill's gun collection . . .
BALL POINT RIFLE, 50¢

About the Author

After playing and working hard, and learning all sorts of things in her parents' restaurant, Stamatina Vavul became a professional oboist.

Unfortunately, that career was short lived as slowly her hands became uncoordinated, and she developed scotomata (blind areas in her vision).

She was finally diagnosed as having Multiple Sclerosis. The diagnosis came during her first year of marriage to Joel Samson. The couple is now in their 39th year of marriage! The couple's twin adult daughters reside near their parent's home. However, the Samsons' home is truly ruled by Giggles, Dr. Samson's assistance dog.

Doctor Samson cannot be held down. Over the years she has held jobs in sales, business management, and retail management. For nine years, she was an entertainment agent and producer, working with ethnic and national performers, conventions, and organizations. She has earned a BA in Communication, a Masters Degree in Rehabilitation

Psychology, and a Ph.D. in Counseling (psychology). Her most meaningful position was, and is, being the head of her own private counseling practice. And, her most prominent achievement was the development of ArtsWORK Indiana, an organization which helps people with disabilities either find positions working in the arts, or become independent artists.

Currently, Dr. Samson uses a voice-operated computer system and telephone, as her hands are quite disabled. Her eyesight is poor, and she uses an electric wheelchair—with which she can control herself and her world. She's a pleasure to visit and speak with.

Dr. Stamatina P. Yocheved Samson has lived a very full life of learning and service, despite her disability. While she is semi-retired, she still has a few patients and is still working at sharing her knowledge and enthusiasm for living a thoughtful life. She maintains a very pleasant disposition, and looks forward to many more productive years.

Source of Gun Identifications

In 2013, Paul Lowe provided as many identifications as he felt sure of, by applying his extensive knowledge to the pictures used in this book. He would have been able to tell more from the real firearms, but sadly, that was not possible.

Many of the weapons shown in this book (especially the derringers), remain unidentified due to a lack of detail in, or the non-revealing angles of, the photographs.

Lowe is a shooter, firearms instructor, licensed firearms dealer, and somewhat of a collector. His interest is mainly in shooting, but he is also interested in vintage rifles---19th and 20th century, mainly military arms.

Lowe says, "I am a student of firearms and I have come to realize that the more I study this field, the more there is I don't know. The research is on-going."

Lowe lives in Buckeye, Arizona, where he has been for most of his life.

Dr. Samson and Rifll Publishing thank Paul Lowe for his contribution to this book.

www.ingramcontent.com/pod-product-compliance
Lightning Source LLC
Chambersburg PA
CBHW05055280326
41933CB00011B/1859